Erik Is Homeless

Erik Is Homeless

Keith Elliot Greenberg

Photographs by Carol Halebian

Lerner Publications Company / Minneapolis

Copyright © 1992 by Lerner Publications Company
All rights reserved. No part of this book may be
reproduced or transmitted in any form or by any means,
electronic or mechanical, including photocopying and
recording, or by any information storage or retrieval
system, without permission in writing from the publisher,
except for the inclusion of brief quotations in an
acknowledged review.

Library of Congress Cataloging-in-Publication Data

Greenberg, Keith Elliot.
    Erik is homeless / Keith Elliot Greenberg ; photographs by Carol Halebian.
        p.   cm.
    Summary: A photographic essay about a nine-year-old boy who is
homeless in New York City.
    ISBN 0-8225-2551-8
    1. Homeless children—New York (N.Y.)—Juvenile literature.
2. Homelessness—New York (N.Y.)—Juvenile literature.
3. Justiniano, Erik. [1. Homeless persons. 2. Homelessness.
3. Justiniano, Erik.] I. Halebian, Carol, ill. II. Title.
HV4506.N6G74   1992
362.7'08'6942—dc20   91-11520
                                                                  CIP
                                                                  AC

Manufactured in the United States of America

1 2 3 4 5 6 7 8 9 10 01 00 99 98 97 96 95 94 93 92

Author's Note

I wish to thank Homes for the Homeless, located at 44 Cooper Square, Suite 3R, New York, NY 10003, for providing access to the residents and counselors at its facilities. Most of the information in this book is the result of interviews conducted specifically for this project. Interviews and photography for this book were completed during the fall and winter of 1990-91.

Last night, Erik watched a horror movie on television. "It was nasty," the nine-year-old remembers, "about a man who robbed graves and cut up the bodies." But, as Erik stretches in bed now at 7:00 A.M., he says he didn't have nightmares.

Erik Justiniano is not easily frightened by movies. Real life has been a lot scarier.

Erik is homeless. He has lived in New York City's crowded public shelters—buildings where dozens of homeless people sleep on beds in the same large room—and in the filthy, dangerous hotels where people without homes of their own can stay. For the last two months, he and his mother, Lydia Oliveras, have been staying in the Prospect Interfaith Family Inn in the South Bronx section of New York City.

For someone who is homeless, the Prospect is a better place to stay than most. It is clean, there are recreational and educational programs for children and adults, and Public School 62 is within walking distance. The people who run the hotel say it offers "transitional housing"—the final step for residents before they move into a real home.

The Prospect is a white brick building that used to be a hospital. Now it is a temporary home for 88 families, including 61 children in either elementary or junior high school. The inn seems more like a public building than a place where people live. The tile floors are mopped regularly by a maintenance crew, and colorful children's paintings hang on the cinder block walls.

Erik and his mother sleep on simple metal frame beds across from each other in what was once a hospital room. There is just one dresser, so they keep most of their clothes in cardboard boxes. A small black-and-white television sits on top of a miniature refrigerator. A sketch that Erik drew of a clown is taped on the wall. The shower is down the hall.

With its long, bare hallways and shiny linoleum floors, the Prospect seems more like a school or hospital than a home.

Beneath a rack of clothing on hangers, Erik's bicycle leans on its kickstand. These days, he doesn't get much of a chance to ride. The South Bronx is one of the most dangerous neighborhoods in the city. Once, Erik's friend was riding his bicycle, and the rear tire popped. The boy mistook the noise for a gunshot and peddled frantically, with a flat tire, back to the Prospect.

9

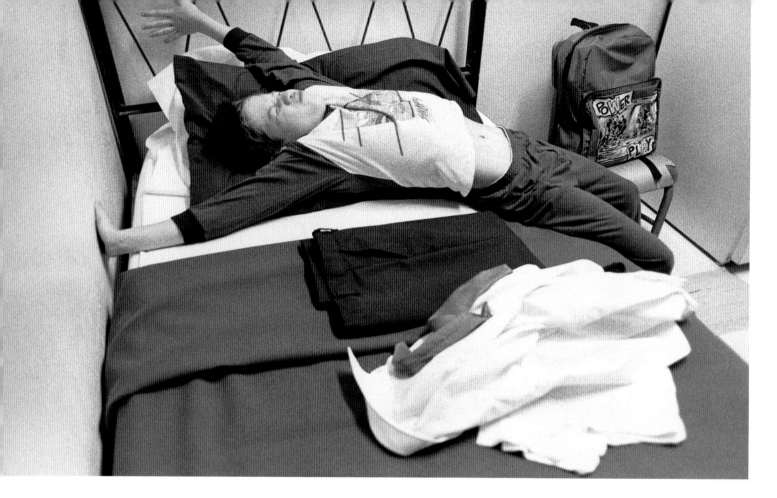

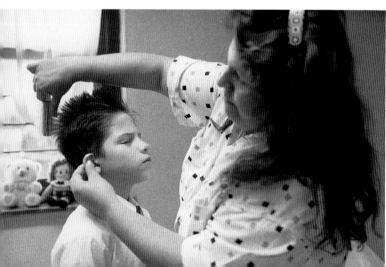

Erik's school requires each student to wear a uniform, but Lydia could not afford the $110 outfit. Instead, she went to a discount clothing store and bought items similar in appearance to the uniform for just $66. This morning she spreads Erik's white shirt, red tie, and blue trousers on his bed. When she gets her next Social Security check, she will buy black shoes to replace the white sneakers her son now wears with the suit.

As Erik buttons up his shirt, his mother runs a comb through his brown hair. Before she became homeless and lost her job, Lydia was a hairdresser. She gave her son a spiky haircut like that of his favorite cartoon character, Bart Simpson, with a little ponytail in the back.

Breakfast is served in a cafeteria in the Prospect's basement. The residents can eat there or bring a tray to their room. Today, Lydia decides on the latter. Erik drinks juice and eats pancakes and sausage while getting ready for school.

The door to their room is open, and from time to time other residents peek in to say hello. Erik and his mom know every face because the Prospect is very strict about letting outsiders into the building. All visitors must sign a guest book, and they are allowed to meet with residents only in the lobby. This helps cut down on the problems that frequently happen at shelters and other facilities for the homeless—problems such as drug dealing and prostitution.

Usually Erik walks to school with some other children from the Prospect. Before he leaves the building, though, he must report to a city Board of Education worker, who keeps a list of all the students staying at the inn. If any of them do not come downstairs to go to school, the worker goes to their rooms to check on them. As a result, children at the Prospect have a nearly perfect attendance rate. Most homeless children in New York City miss school about half the time. They might miss school because they move around so much, or because their parents are busy trying to find a job or a place to live.

As he leaves the inn, Erik looks both ways. He is checking to make sure none of his schoolmates are around. The other pupils in Erik's third-grade class do not know that he is homeless, and he wants to keep it that way. Occasionally, school friends have asked to come over to his house. "I tell them I live far away," Erik says. "Then they don't have to find out where I live."

Sometimes Lydia accompanies her son to the large, red brick school building. The streets are quiet this morning, but Lydia keeps a close eye on her son. One of the run-down buildings along the route is a hangout for drug dealers. Erik assures her that she has nothing to worry about. "I don't know how anybody can take drugs," he says. "Drugs kill you."

Sometimes Lydia walks with Erik to his school. She worries about the dangerous neighborhood.

Erik is more concerned about a large black dog with clumps of fur missing. The dog wanders the sidewalks looking hungry, and one time it growled at Erik and a friend, forcing them to leap onto a parked car.

As Lydia stands in the corner of the schoolyard, watching her son line up with his class, her heart skips a beat. Her cousin is walking toward her with a big smile on his face! Lydia likes her cousin, but he does not know that she and Erik are homeless.

"You're living around here now?" he asks in a friendly tone.

"Yes," she answers cautiously. "What are you doing here?"

"I'm applying for a job as a math teacher."

Lydia wishes him luck, then looks away nervously. Her cousin leaves, and she focuses on Erik and his class, filing into the school building. She hasn't given away her secret, but she wishes she had a real home. Then she and Erik would not feel ashamed.

In the schoolyard, Erik's mother adjusts his shirt before he goes in.

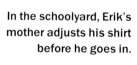

14

I t's hard to say exactly how many people are homeless. According to the National Coalition for the Homeless, somewhere between 500,000 and 3 million Americans are without a home. Perhaps as many as a million of them are children.

New York City, where Erik lives, has been hit particularly hard. Between 1981 and 1988, the number of homeless families rose by more than 500 percent, according to Homes for the Homeless, an organization that helps people like Erik and his mother find permanent homes. In 1990, 3,800 homeless families, including 11,000 children, were being housed in city-run shelters or hotels. Ralph Nunez, president of Homes for the Homeless, estimated that, in addition, 12,000 individuals were in shelters. About 10,000 others were living on New York's streets.

The reasons for homelessness are many and complicated. Contributing to the problem are poverty, rising rents and lack of low-income housing, drug and alcohol abuse, and cuts in social programs that help poor people. About 25 percent of the homeless are mentally ill. After they are released from hospitals or treatment centers, many former patients have trouble finding jobs and homes, and they are forced to live on the streets.

Nunez traces the problem in New York to the early 1980s, when the federal government cut housing funds for the poor. Low-income families discovered that there were few apartments in their price range. Many low-income families began doubling up, with two families sharing the same apartment. Eventually, some of those people became homeless.

To many of us, homelessness is an annoyance. We don't like to see homeless people lined along the walls of train stations or subways, or on the street, covered with dirt, wrapped in rags, or sleeping on cardboard or plastic. While the homeless are not always feared, they are frequently scorned. It is common to hear people say that the homeless simply don't like to work, that they brought their problems on themselves.

In Penn Station and many other places in New York City, homeless people are a common sight. Commuters usually walk right by them.

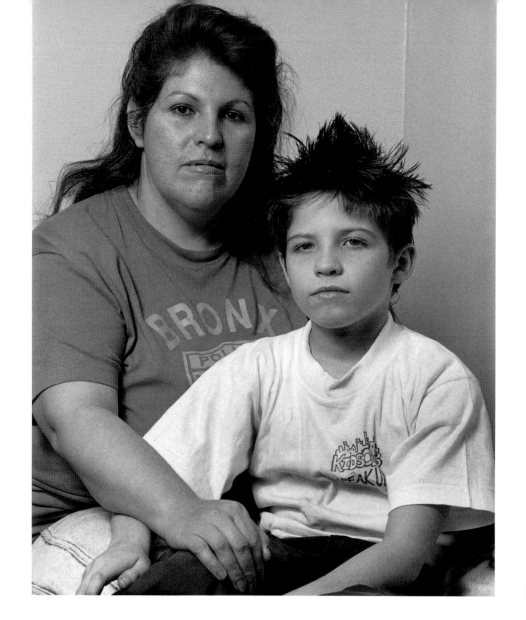

Lydia and Erik

Erik's mother, Lydia Oliveras, never wanted to be homeless. And she did not avoid finding a job.

Until 1985, Erik was part of an average, middle-class family. His father, Gino Justiniano, was a plumber. Lydia worked as a hairdresser. Along with her children from a previous marriage—a 10-year-old boy and 15-year-old girl—they lived in a two-bedroom apartment in the New York City suburb of White Plains. The hard-working Gino never had problems paying their $790 monthly rent. Business was so good that the family had two cars, an Oldsmobile and a Cadillac.

On November 14, 1985, Gino, a diabetic, was driving home when he started to feel weak. He had been working long hours—six days a week and Sundays when emergencies arose—and neglecting his diet. He pulled his car over on a Bronx street and started walking toward a grocery. As he crossed the street, a car smashed into him.

Lydia was at home when the police arrived. They told her that her husband had been in an accident but they would not provide more details. It was only when she arrived at Montefiore Hospital in the Bronx that she learned that medics had found Gino dead at the scene.

She tried to explain to Erik, who was then four years old, what had happened. "He was small," Lydia remembers. "He didn't understand."

Since her husband was the family's main provider, she began to work double shifts, hoping to increase her $280 weekly salary. Her mother baby-sat, but it bothered Lydia that she rarely saw her children.

After struggling for more than a year, Lydia realized that she and her family could no longer afford to stay in their apartment. Her mother asked them to move in with her, but Lydia wanted to manage on her own. A temporary solution was a Bronx apartment a friend made available for $300 a month. But after a year and a half, the friend needed the apartment again, and Lydia's family had to move out. Lydia looked all over the city, but she could not find a place she could afford.

The family split up. Erik's half-brother went to live with his natural father. His half-sister found a high-paying job in Atlantic City, New Jersey. Lydia and Erik moved into a shelter for the homeless in March 1990.

"I'm still depressed about it," Lydia admits. "I know that I've tried hard for my kids, but I can't help feeling like I let them down."

Erik and his mother were shuttled through 10 city-run hotels and 2 shelters within 6 months. The constant moving forced Lydia to keep quitting jobs. Soon she was unemployed. Erik had to change schools three times in one year. He fell behind in his studies and was left back in the third grade. To make matters worse, Lydia slipped on some stairs at one of the hotels and broke several teeth.

One of their most terrifying experiences was a stay at the Auburn Hotel in Brooklyn. Their room was burglarized twice, so Lydia had to push a heavy dresser against the door each night before they went to sleep. After Erik found crack vials and condoms in the bathroom, he refused to take a shower without his mother standing guard. Another time, he saw two women fighting over drugs in the cafeteria.

Lydia went to a counselor at the hotel. "Please get me out of here," she begged. "I never imagined that these types of things went on."

Four days later, they moved into the Prospect.

Opposite: Erik and his mother talk with a social worker at the Prospect. They were lucky—and grateful—to get a room at the inn. Above: Erik plays with other kids in the shelter's playroom.

Homes for the Homeless runs three centers in New York City— one of them is the Prospect. While many facilities for the homeless offer little or no individual attention, adults at the Prospect are encouraged to participate in classes about finding and keeping an apartment, and, if necessary, drug and alcohol rehabilitation. Children can take art classes, play sports, receive tutoring to improve their grades, and study musical instruments.

The classes offered at the inn have made Erik more enthusiastic about school. He's thought about becoming a math teacher, even though he sometimes forgets his multiplication tables.

His favorite subject is art. Drawing seems to come naturally to Erik. He puts the pencil to the paper and pictures just appear. Helen Schmidt, the Prospect's family counselor, says a love of art is common among homeless children. "They've been through so much, and now they use their experiences to create," she says. "They're very expressive."

Erik likes drawing because he can make whatever he wants. "You can draw whatever is on your mind and make it real," he says.

Several years ago, Erik visited relatives in Puerto Rico (Lydia was born in Puerto Rico), and he saw the way the rich people lived there. Now he draws a mansion. "I can't wait until I grow up," he says. "I'll live in a big house with a swimming pool, and I'll have a house for my mother, too."

Like young people everywhere, homeless children have big dreams, but the challenges they face in school are unique. Helen Schmidt observes that many of them have trouble concentrating. "By moving around so much, they keep getting transferred to different schools, sometimes missing a week or two of classes in between."

She says the children often fall behind in their schoolwork, and they don't have time to make friends with other kids or grow close to teachers. "Then, in the noisy public shelters, doing homework or studying is next to impossible."

Erik takes an art class at the Bronx Museum. He sketches one of the paintings in the museum, then shows it to his teacher.

Erik takes a break from his homework at the city park.

Israel Figueroa, director of education at the Prospect, says that homeless children may seem shy to their classmates. "They don't trust people. They're fearful. When someone tries to get close to them, they back away."

Many are embarrassed about being homeless. Some of the students from the Prospect leave school with their classmates and walk in the opposite direction of the inn, turning back only after the other students are out of sight.

26

Erik has been taunted on his way home from school by a group of neighborhood kids who hang out near the Prospect. These kids tease Erik and his friends about their hand-me-down clothes and about being homeless.

"A homeless kid is just a kid like anyone else," Erik complains. "People who make fun of us should learn their manners. What if they become homeless one day? They won't like it if we make fun of them."

Opposite: One of the
"homework helper"
assistants helps Erik
with his assignment.

Israel Figueroa has heard all the stories about homeless children being teased. He runs the "homework helper" program at the Prospect and often talks with Erik and the other children when they return from school.

"Don't waste your time with those other kids," he advises them. "They're ignorant... If they tease you, ignore them and keep on walking. They're not important. Your schoolwork is. That's what'll make your dreams come true."

The homework helper program is what you might imagine it to be—the children go to a special room in the Prospect each afternoon to do their homework, and Israel and his assistants help them with their questions. The students are not allowed to leave until they've completed their assignments.

Today Erik is copying a list of new spelling words in his notebook. Nearby, an older boy struggles with fractions. At another table, a kindergarten girl is learning to read.

Erik works on multiplication tables with his teacher.

Erik's work isn't exactly easy, but he sticks with it. He and his mother have talked many times about the importance of education, and he realizes that completing his homework is the first step to achieving success later in life.

"You can't get a good job without a good education," Erik says. "That's something my mother always tells me, and I know it's true."

Sometimes he talks about being a math teacher, but other times Erik thinks he'd like to be a lawyer. "A lawyer makes a lot of money, but he also helps people who need him," he explains, "people who've lost their homes and don't have money. I'd like to change that. People need money for clothes and food. They need a place to live, and they need people like lawyers to help them."

After finishing his homework, Erik stops by the medical van. Since 1987, a group of New York doctors has been helping the homeless by bringing a medical van to shelters and hotels around the city. On Thursdays, it stops at the Prospect, along with a dental van. The doctors provide services free of charge. One doctor observes that many homeless children suffer from heart murmurs, dehydration, asthma, and ear infections—conditions that result from a lack of regular health care.

Above: Erik and other homeless children enjoy a pizza break during a field trip. Opposite: The kids also picked pumpkins and visited an old-fashioned gristmill, where a guide in costume gave them a tour.

Erik has been able to get outside of the city on trips that a New York company sponsors for homeless children. He has been on picnics, petted animals at a farm, picked pumpkins, and visited an old-fashioned gristmill, where grain is ground. He likes the chance to get away from the noise and crime of his neighborhood.

A globe brings geography into perspective for the students at the Brownstone School.

Dinner is hot dogs, baked beans, and a container of milk. Erik again brings the meal to his room and eats quickly, because the Brownstone School starts at 6:00 P.M.

The Brownstone School is in the same room as the homework helper program, but its purpose is slightly different. While the homework helper program assists the child with his or her schoolwork, the Brownstone School tries to find the children's strong areas—in math, science, or literature—and build on them.

"Many of these kids have talent, but that talent has not been noticed because of their environment," says Jim King, coordinator of the Brownstone School. "Because of their circumstances, they might act up a little in school, and they are treated like there's something wrong with them. We not only try to tell them they're fine, we try to recognize the children who are gifted."

Erik concentrates on improving his basic abilities, figuring out multiplication tables and trying to raise his reading level. King hopes the personal attention offered to Erik at the Brownstone School will help him keep up with his classmates.

Meanwhile, Erik's mother is also working on improving her situation. Several months ago, she took a test to become a corrections officer (someone who works in a prison). She scored 87 out of 100, even though she does not have a high school diploma. Corrections officers must be high school graduates, so Lydia is taking a class to get her diploma while she waits to be called for duty. Her English is pretty good (it is her second language), but she is still working to improve her grammar. She also plans to have dental work done on her chipped teeth.

"I'm very hopeful," she says. "It's tough, but I feel we're on our way. I'm never going to let this situation happen again."

Lydia expects to begin looking for an apartment soon. Counselors from Homes for the Homeless will continue to check on the family for a year after they've settled into a home, to make sure they can handle the problems that will likely occur, away from the security of the inn.

The average person stays at a place like the Prospect Inn for six months. The positive side of the experience is that the residents can take advantage of the many free, helpful programs that are not often available to poor people who do have homes.

The future for Erik and his mother looks fairly good. Only six percent of Homes for the Homeless graduates become homeless again after finding a new place, according to director Ralph Nunez. Unfortunately, the figure is higher for other homeless people in New York City—40 percent.

Lydia attends a class that helps her develop the skills she needs to find an apartment and a job.

It's late now, and Erik is lying on his bed in his pajamas, going over his spelling words again. Lydia sits on her bed across from him, reading a high school English book.

"I know you're going to be somebody," she looks up and tells her son.

"You don't have to tell me," he jokes. "I know."

Smiling, Erik closes his book, puts it away, slides under the covers, and shuts his eyes.

He does not expect to have any nightmares tonight.

For Further Reading

Beckelman, Laurie. *The Homeless.* New York: Crestwood House, 1989.

Hahn, Mary Downing. *December Stillness.* New York: Avon, 1988.

Kenyon, Thomas L., and Justine Blau. *What You Can Do to Help the Homeless.* New York: Simon & Schuster, 1991.

Kosof, Anna. *Homeless in America.* New York: Franklin Watts, 1988.

Kozol, Jonathan. *Rachel and Her Children.* New York: Crown Pub., 1988.

Landau, Elaine. *The Homeless.* New York: Julian Messner, 1987.

O'Connor, Karen. *Homeless Children.* San Diego: Lucent Books, 1989.

Orr, Lisa, ed. *The Homeless: Opposing Viewpoints.* San Diego: Greenhaven Press, 1990.

Stavsky, Lois, and I. E. Mozeson, eds. *The Place I Call Home: Voices and Faces of Homeless Teens.* New York: Shapolsky Pub., 1991.

Resources

The Homeless Information Exchange
1830 Connecticut Ave. NW
Fourth Floor
Washington, DC 20009

National Alliance to End Homelessness
1518 K St. NW, Suite 206
Washington, DC 20005

National Coalition for the Homeless
1439 Rhode Island Ave. NW
Washington, DC 20005

Afterword

Six months after this book was written, Erik and Lydia were on their way to putting homelessness behind them. The two had moved into their own apartment in the South Bronx. Although the neighborhood has many problems, the building they live in is clean and modern. Erik has his own room, and there is even a bunk bed so friends can sleep over.

In the meantime, Lydia has found a new boyfriend. They are planning to marry soon.

Because of the educational programs at the Prospect, Erik had his best school year ever.

"The worst days are over," Lydia says. "Thank God."

Sadly, for many homeless people, the outlook is not so bright. Find out what you can do in your community to help the homeless.